The 11 Things Your Kids Should Know

(So They Can Save America)

The 11 Things Your Kids Should Know

(So They Can Save America)

~

And Basic Lessons for the Rest of Us

Steve White

iUniverse, Inc.
Bloomington

The 11 Things Your Kids Should Know (So They Can Save America) And Basic Lessons for the Rest of Us

iUniverse books may be ordered through booksellers or by contacting:

iUniverse
1663 Liberty Drive
Bloomington, IN 47403
www.iuniverse.com
1-800-Authors (1-800-288-4677)

Because of the dynamic nature of the Internet, any web addresses or links contained in this book may have changed since publication and may no longer be valid. The views expressed in this work are solely those of the author and do not necessarily reflect the views of the publisher, and the publisher hereby disclaims any responsibility for them.

Any people depicted in stock imagery provided by Thinkstock are models, and such images are being used for illustrative purposes only.

Certain stock imagery © Thinkstock.

ISBN: 978-1-4697-6914-1 (sc)
ISBN: 978-1-4697-6915-8 (e)

Library of Congress Control Number: 2012901943

Printed in the United States of America

iUniverse rev. date: 02/29/2012

For my grandchildren and all of my
unborn great grandchildren.

Contents

Preface

In my previous book entitled *Please Change Your Mind*, I created a graphic diagram that showed how the mind works. A brief summary of that graphic is provided here and will be helpful to you in understanding *The 11 Things Your Kids Should Know*.

Life comes at all of us at 100 mph every day, whether we like it or not. You process life through a lens. On that lens, you place laws, which are simply the rules that you hold to be true. They only get there with your permission. Laws are suggested from many different places like parents, school, church, and your own experiences. But ultimately, you have to approve them before they go on your lens.

You have these laws about virtually everything, such as the following:

- Men not crying.
- Mom's way to do the laundry.

- Dad's way to park the car.
- My self-worth being dependent on winning at games.
- And on and on and on.

You have these laws about every aspect of your life. When something happens in your life, you process it through your lens, which contains all your laws. At the same time, you, like everyone else, have a set of human needs that you're trying to meet.

So when something happens in life, the first thing you do is think something. What you think is driven by the laws on your lens. If, for example, you have a law on your lens that says, "Dogs are vicious," then whenever you see a dog you will think, "This dog is vicious." Once you think that, you will feel something, which in this case is probably fear. If you feel fear, then what are you likely to do? Run, of course. And this is the progression for everything that occurs in your life: you think something, you feel something, and then you do something.

The things that you do, your behavior, will create results in your life. These results will either meet your needs or they won't. But results take time to measure. So if over time your results are not meeting your needs, then you probably have a bad law on your lens. Human growth is the process of examining the laws on your lens and changing the ones that aren't meeting your needs. Your *epicenter of control* is in what you *think*. And if you can change what you *think,* then you change everything.

I'm not saying that *your* laws are good or bad or right or wrong. All I'm saying is that you have a lens, that you are putting laws on your lens every day, and that you hold these laws to be true. Your laws dictate what you think, which drives what you feel, which in turn drives what you do. What you do creates results in your life. Those results produce feedback that either meets your needs or doesn't.

In diagram form, the process looks like this:

The *PLEASE CHANGE YOUR MIND* Process

The 11 Things Your Kids Should Know (So They Can Save America) are the eleven laws that I would put on the lens of every child. And when I say *laws,* I mean collectively all the things that we might call principles, beliefs, or things that we hold to be true.

Introduction

I came to understand how my mind really works late in my life. I developed the *Please Change Your Mind* process diagram long after it had any chance of impacting the lives of my children.

At the same time, I am becoming increasingly convinced that the United States of America is in big trouble. Since our Founding Fathers wrote the Declaration of Independence and crafted our Constitution, our nation seems to have lost its moral compass and its sense of right and wrong. It is essential that we reclaim these virtues.

Our country has huge issues to deal with today, not the least of which are our $14 trillion debt, immigration, extreme terrorist groups, foreign wars, entitlement programs that are unsustainable, and unemployment. On top of all these issues, we have a Congress today filled with career politicians—Republicans and Democrats—who seem more interested in getting reelected than in doing what is right for our country.

But I see these problems as the symptom and not the cause. The cause is this: for over two hundred years, we, as individuals, have slowly lost our moral compass. Today we lack the honesty, integrity, and, most of all, the moral values of our forefathers.

If you don't believe me, just look at the things that characterize our society today: pornography, drug use, prostitution, abortion, fatherlessness, child abuse, profanity, lying, cheating, and stealing. Our prisons are full, our education system is woefully behind global standards, divorce is skyrocketing, and we've generally created a mess for the next generation to fix.

But all these problems aren't the fault of our country or our government. They're our fault.

You see, the government doesn't need fixing. People need fixing.

So I got to thinking. What if I could start over and put the most important laws on the lenses of my children? What would they be? What laws would I try to influence and encourage them to adopt? What laws would have the most impact on their lives and create the most personal fulfillment for them? What laws would reset their moral compass and sense of right and wrong to those of our forefathers?

So I started making a list. It turns out that I identified eleven essential principles. Then it occurred to me that all my grandchildren still had time to influence all my unborn great grandchildren. What if they could raise up a generation that embodied the same principles as our Founding Fathers? What if *you* could raise up *your* children with those principles? Our kids are our lineage and we want the best for them. But they could also be the ones to save America—because if we can change the people, we will change the country.

So I decided to write this book for you and your children, plus all my unborn family and all future Americans, in the hope that they will be the difference. If we succeed at instilling these principles in our children, as they were in our Founding Fathers, then I believe that all the big governmental problems facing America today will eventually fix themselves.

My credentials for writing this book are no more than yours. I'm just a concerned citizen, of a nation in trouble, who has raised four children of his own. So this book is just my opinion. It is not founded on any scientific research or proven facts. You be the judge of its validity.

I'm starting today to instill these eleven principles in my entire family. If you happen to agree, then I welcome you and your family to join us and be a part of this road to recovery. Together we must make a difference.

A Few Words
about Parenting

Before we start on the eleven things, I want to say a few words about families and parenting in general. Over the last one hundred years or so, it seems to me that there has been a continual breakdown of the family unit. Even the best intended families are so busy, with such diverse schedules, that it is now rare for them to even have dinner together.

Over the same period, there also seems to have been an erosion of quality parenting. And believe me: I see myself as part of this phenomenon. With a struggling economy, many families now have both parents working, and kids are either in day care or after-school programs. This is not to mention the number of single moms and dads who struggle to balance work with parenting and raising families. The bottom line, for all the reasons, is that our kids have gotten the short end of the stick.

We just simply have to do better! Our kids are the future of our nation. We have created a mess for them. Fixing the mess, in my opinion, starts with being better parents and teaching our children to do better than we did.

It is my opinion that parenting is *the* most difficult job in the world. And the irony is that it is also the job for which you receive the least training. Suddenly one day you just are one. Nobody ever sat you down and told you the dos and don'ts of parenting. Stephen Covey didn't write a book called *The 7 Habits of Highly Effective Parents*. The only things that we really have to draw on are our own perceptions of what our parents did that we considered right or wrong. Welcome to the toughest job in the world.

Just think—you brought another life into the world. And it is now your responsibility to prepare that child for anything and everything he or she is going to face in life. And you've only got about eighteen years to do it. A simply daunting task.

As parents, you're demonstrating your value system to your children every day. They listen to what you say (most of the time), but they also watch everything you do. I'd like to share an anonymous poem called "A Father and His Son," which can be found at www.TheInspirationPlace.com/poems. It applies equally to moms and daughters as well.

There are little eyes upon you
And they're watching night and day.

There are little ears that quickly
Take in every word you say.

There are little hands all eager
To do everything you do.
And a little boy who's dreaming
Of the day he'll be like you.

You're the little fellow's idol,
You're the wisest of the wise.
In his little mind about you
No suspicions ever rise.

He believes in you devoutly;
Holds that all you say and do
He will say and do in your way
When he's grown up just like you.

There's a wide-eyed little fellow
Who believes you're always right,
And his ears are always open
And he watches day and night.

You are setting an example
Every day in all you do.
For the little boy who's waiting
To grow up and be like you.

Author Unknown

You are always on display for them. You're never off stage.

Pretty soon they grow up and become teenagers. The most dangerous thing that teens do is make decisions. So before they get to be teens, it is essential that they have a lot of experience with decision-making. The way you do that is to let them make a lot of decisions. You let three-year-olds make three-year-old's decisions on things that have little if any consequence—like what to wear. Who cares?

The early years are also when you'll teach them the most about character traits. They learn this by watching you. Are you honest, generous, thoughtful, and loving? Are you a person of integrity with high moral standards? Do you treat people with respect? Are you fair? Do you care about the feelings of others? They will see all this in your life, and they'll put laws on their lenses commensurate with what they see in you. The character traits that you want for your children should also be specific topics of discussion and not just what they observe. Tell them the lifelong benefits; tell them that it will best meet their needs over time. And always remember what Martin Buxbaum said in a line from his poem entitled *Success*:

> The measure of real success
> Is one you cannot spend.
> It's the way your child describes you
> When talking to a friend.

As they get older, you let them make decisions commensurate with their age. The consequences get more significant, and your job is to explain the consequences to them but let the decisions be theirs. You train them to analyze each decision and anticipate the consequences, positive or negative, before they decide. They will make mistakes—that's how they learn. Your job is to make sure that no decision is beyond their capability to assess the consequences and that no life-altering decisions get made.

Then, when they go off to college and really *are* on their own, they have years of training in decision-making. And they've demonstrated that they're capable of making good decisions. You can then trust them to make good future decisions.

There are three other things to know about parenting:

1. The hardest part of raising children is teaching them to ride a bicycle. You can either run beside the bicycle or stand and yell directions while the child falls. A shaky child on a bicycle needs both freedom and support. The tricky part is realizing that is what they'll always need.
2. It's impossible to treat a child too well. Children are spoiled by being ignored too much or by harshness, not by kindness. Rich kids are often spoiled not by their toys and automobiles but by parents who are too busy to pay any attention to them.

3. Children grow up and go away to live their own lives at about age eighteen. Parents who accept this as a natural part of the order of things will see their grown children surprisingly often.

So let's teach our kids about the value of family; the value of positive character traits like honesty, integrity, and fairness; and the values of our forefathers who founded this nation.

Chapter 1

Make Sure They Like That Person in the Mirror

It is absolutely essential that your kids like themselves. But they are complex, and there are many component parts that make up their personality. So in order for them to like themselves, they have to like all their component parts. Some of their component parts include their morals, values, ethics, and personal integrity.

Webster defines morals as motivation based on your ideas of right or wrong. So how do your kids decide what is right or wrong? Like most kids, you play the biggest part in helping them form their concepts of right and wrong. But even in an environment without parental guidance, kids can ask themselves two questions: Does it hurt anybody else, and would I hate this to be done to me? If the answer is yes to either question, then it is probably wrong and they shouldn't do it.

1

Values are a little different. Values are more beliefs in which they have an emotional investment. Things that they value don't necessarily have anything to do with right or wrong. For example, their highest value could be education, whereas someone else's highest value could be health. Neither is necessarily right or wrong, just different. And they could both value health and education—just on different levels. But again, my litmus test for values is whether or not what they do hurts other people and whether they would want that action to happen to themselves. I believe that the best source for further personal guidance on the appropriateness of your morals and values, your sense of right and wrong, can be found in the Bible. Some examples are found below.

- **Morals and Values** – See Exodus 23:24–25, Judges 8:31, 2 Samuel 3:7, 2 Chronicles 13:8, 1 Corinthians 6:19–20, Romans 1:25 and 12:3, Ephesians 2:3, and Philippians 1:20–21.
- **Integrity** – See Genesis 43:12, Psalms 25:21, Proverbs 19:1 and 12:3, Matthew 3:15, and Luke 16:10–11.
- **Right/Wrong** – See Exodus 20:1–17.

Ethics is yet another component part of your kids. *Webster* defines ethics as the philosophical study of moral values and rules and motivation based on your ideas of right and wrong. Ethics is not only found at the personal level but also at the corporate level. Corporations and even Congress have ethics committees to monitor behavior and ensure that people conduct themselves appropriately. On a personal level, it is simply doing what is right and fair. I have a good friend who has a tagline on all his e-mails. It says, "Do the Right Thing, and Do It Right Now." That's a good description of ethics in action.

Now we come to personal integrity. *Webster's* definition of integrity is the quality, or state of being, of sound moral principle; uprightness, honesty, and sincerity. Personal integrity includes morals, values, and ethics, but it goes beyond those to include honesty and sincerity. Our kids should be people of their word. When they tell someone that they will do something, they should make sure that they do it. When they tell someone they will be there, make sure that they show up. And if they told them a time, then they should be on time. Their word should be like money in the bank. People should know that they can always count on our kids because they are people of their word.

In addition to these components that make up our kids, there are others worthy of consideration as well. I cannot spend time on all the components, but there are many pieces that make up their character, components that define who they really are. Our kids need to examine them all and be the best people that they can possibly be.

In addition to the component parts, they also have many aspects to their lives. These aspects include family, school, church, work, recreation, and so on. We each have many aspects to our lives, and we bring our character to each and every one.

One thing they need is congruence. They must agree with themselves. By that, I mean congruence between the three basic activities in life—thinking, saying, and doing. If what they think, what they say, and what they do are all in agreement, then there will be a sense of peace and contentment for them. If any activity is incongruent, then they will have a sense of incompleteness, deception, and a lack of fulfillment. *Practice what you preach* is a great motto for them.

So how do they really know if they like that person in the mirror or not? What's their basis for determining what criteria they should they use? How do they do it? Socrates gave us the answer. He said, "A life unexamined is not worth living." I believe that; I think they must examine themselves. They should examine themselves by asking four basic questions:

- Are all my component parts (values, morals, ethics, and personal integrity) where I want them to be? Am I a person of good character?
- Am I applying my character across all the aspects of my life?
- Is there congruence between what I think, what I say, and what I do?
- How do I measure up in the other ten chapters of this book?

If they like their answers to these questions, then I am confident that they will like that person in the mirror. If they don't like their answers, then make sure they fix any inconsistencies immediately. Do not let them wait until tomorrow. Putting off the change will only make it more difficult for them to fix later.

Peter "Dale" Wimbrow wrote a poem in 1934 that sums it up very nicely:

The Guy in the Glass

When you get what you want in your struggle for pelf,
And the world makes you king for a day,
Then go to the mirror and look at yourself,
And see what *that* guy has to say.

For it isn't your Father, or Mother, or Wife,
Who judgment upon you must pass.
The feller whose verdict counts most in your life
Is the guy staring back from the glass.

He's the feller to please, never mind all the rest,
For he's with you clear to the end,
And you've passed your most dangerous, difficult test
If the guy in the glass is your friend.

You may be like Jack Horner and "chisel" a plum,
And think you're a wonderful guy,

But the man in the glass says you're only a bum
If you can't look him straight in the eye.

You may fool the whole world down the pathway of years,
And get pats on the back as you pass,
But your final reward will be heartache and tears,
If you've cheated the guy in the glass.

(This poem can be found at www.theguyintheglass.com/gig.htm.)

As adults, what you do will speak more loudly than anything you say. Our kids are looking to us as examples. If they don't see these attributes in your life, then how can you expect to see them in their lives? Kids see honesty, integrity, moral values, and separating right from wrong in the things we do every day. Kids will know whether there is incongruence in your life, and they will know whether *you* like the person in *your* mirror.

Law number one: Make sure they like that person in the mirror.

Chapter 2

Teach Them to Love Until It Doesn't Hurt Anymore

What a challenge it is to write about love. It is a most difficult word to get your head around. In English, the word *love* can refer to a variety of different feelings, states, and attitudes ranging from generic pleasure ("I love ice cream") to intense interpersonal pleasure ("I love my wife"). Love can be an emotion of strong personal attachment, and love can be a virtue representing all human kindness, compassion, and affection. Love is central to many religions, like "God is love." Love is both a noun and a verb. It can be something you feel as well as something you do. Love can be familial like emotional closeness to family, it can be platonic as in friendships, and it can be religious as in profound oneness with God.

Love in its various forms acts as a major facilitator of interpersonal relationships and, because of its central psychological importance, it is one of the most common themes in the arts. At the same time, science defines love as an evolved state of survival instinct that is primarily used to facilitate the continuation of our species through reproduction. This diversity of uses and meanings, combined with the complexity of feelings involved, makes *love* unusually difficult to consistently define.

We can have love for things like clothes, cars, jewelry, houses, or food, but that kind of love is different from the love we have for people. And while different from the love of things, the love of people varies—like the love we have for a spouse, child, family member, or neighbor. They are all very different from each other. We can also have love for intangibles like our jobs or our looks and for activities like baseball, gardening, or reading.

I believe that there is no greater force in the world than love. So I say—*love*. Make it a verb. Make it something your kids do. Tell them to love everybody and everything. Nobody ever went wrong by loving too much. But many people regret not having loved enough.

I heard a preacher one time delivering a sermon on giving. He said to give. He said to then keep giving until it hurt. Then he said to keep giving until it didn't hurt anymore. He was right. And the same is true for love. Love, like giving, becomes a habit. Love trumps pain. After a while, the pain goes away and only the love remains.

And if they love long enough, they will experience pain, just like you probably did. Tell them to love anyway. They will get over the pain. They may get hurt time and time again. Tell them to keep loving. They are not in control of what other people do, but they are in control of how they feel about it and what they do about it. So tell them to keep on loving until it doesn't hurt anymore. Tell them to love even when it might not seem like the right thing to do. More important than any pain is for them to like that person in the mirror.

I believe that the *action* of love creates a blissful feeling with the same name, and that when the action stops, the blissful feeling goes away. I believe that everyone is capable of loving and of being loved. I also believe that the opposite of love is not hate but fear, which will generate hate, greed, or jealousy. Your kids cannot love and fear at the same time. Have them consider love as the base of the pyramid in all their relationships, and they can build other things upon it.

They have to start by loving themselves. And I don't mean this in a negative, narcissistic way but as an acceptance of themselves. They have to have congruence between what they believe and what they do in order to see themselves as lovable. If they can't honestly see themselves as lovable, then they will have trouble giving or receiving love from others.

I have observed others whom I consider to be really *in love*, as evidenced by their staying together for decades. The major characteristic I see is action—not just feeling. Some of the things I have observed these couples doing are as follows.

- They do things for the other person even when they don't feel like it.
- They go out of their way to do things to make others happy or to help others just feel good.
- They allow the other person space to do his or her thing.
- Each person does not insist on getting his or her own way.
- All their actions are courteous and considerate.
- They look out for the other's interests.
- They control their anger toward one another.
- They take no pleasure in the other's disappointments.
- They have complete trust in one another.
- Their love is unconditional.
- They look toward the future together, beyond their current circumstances, with hope and anticipation.

My other personal advice for you and your kids about love includes the following:

- Never ask for love. Just give it. Expect nothing in return. Therefore, when your children receive love, they will know immediately that it was something the other person wanted to give them.

- Never force love; it will come to them if they can risk giving it away without expectation.
- Teach them to say "I love you" often and mean it by showing it through their actions.
- Have them always put themselves in the shoes of others and try to see things from the other's perspective.
- Have them make it unconditional. If it isn't, it isn't really love but some form of opportunism on their part.
- Assure them that love can be lost and that they should never take it for granted.

As a Christian, the ultimate authority on love for me is the Bible. Interestingly enough, the Bible has a lot to say about love. It teaches that love came from God because God *is* love. Being created in His image, we are endowed with the capacity to love and be loved. According to the Bible, love is caring in action, not something we feel but something we do.

Probably the most familiar scripture about love in the Bible is chapter 13 of First Corinthians, which seems to be read at every wedding I attend. In this chapter, the apostle Paul tells us sixteen things about God's perspective on what love is and what love is not. Read it sometime. Then read it to your kids.

Love is important to God. Paul says in that same chapter that if we could speak every language, but didn't have love, that we would only be like a clanging cymbal. If we could predict the future, know the answer to every mystery, had all knowledge, and had faith that could move mountains but didn't have love, then we would be *nothing!* If we gave everything we had to the poor and were willing to die but didn't have love, we would gain nothing in God's sight.

God certainly places a high importance on love. Love comes from the heart. Solomon said in the book of Proverbs, "Above all else, guard your heart, for it is the wellspring of life." Then Jesus said, "Store up treasure in heaven, for where your treasure is, there will your heart be also." Our hearts, and the love that emanates from them, are of paramount importance to God. In fact, Jesus said that all the laws of the Old Testament could be summarized in two statements:

- Love the Lord with all your heart, soul, mind, and strength.
- Love your neighbor as yourself.

That's it. That's all of the laws in the Old Testament summed up in two statements about love. Pretty incredible!

Make sure that your kids feel your unconditional love. It is essential. I grew up in a home where I believed love was conditional on my performance. In order for me to be loved, I had to get good grades in school, obey all my parents' rules, and display good behavior. I spent my whole childhood exchanging "good boy" for love. Don't be like that.

Make sure your children know that you love them unconditionally, especially when they're bad. What you don't like is their behavior, but you love them. Make that distinction. They are not their behavior or their grades. They are special. They are your children. Love them unconditionally. And make sure they feel it. Ask them often if they know that they are loved unconditionally. What good does it do to love your children unconditionally if they don't feel that love?

Law number two: Teach them to love until it doesn't hurt anymore.

Chapter 3

Teach Them to Be Nice

Nice means exhibiting courtesy and politeness, being pleasant and pleasing and agreeable in nature. Have you ever been around an old scrooge? Ever been around someone who is never happy, always complaining, and always in a bad mood? It was miserable, wasn't it? Don't let your kids become that person.

America seems angry to me. Too many Americans attack people, and often they do so with lies and misguided opinions. We dismiss people, we get angry, and we engage in horrible name-calling. Why? I think people are frustrated. Many are out of work, have lost their homes to foreclosure, or are generally just afraid of an uncertain future. There is ample reinforcement for their position on TV and the Internet, including social media and endless blogs.

If your children want to get people to buy their arguments or their ideas, they will be much more effective and successful if they're nice. Your kids need to know that. Linda Kaplan Thaler and Robin Koval, authors of *The Power of Nice* (New York: Doubleday, 2006), claim that being nice pays off for both you and others. They point to research that shows nice people live longer, are healthier, are luckier in love, make more money, and experience less litigation.

Being nice means using small kindnesses, such as smiles, gestures, compliments, and favors, in all our interactions with people. Your kids need to know that.

Sometimes just being nice will open doors, improve a relationship, and maybe let you sleep better. Being nice means being kind. Being nice means not being phony but being genuine and authentic. Being nice means treating others with compassion and empathy. Your kids need to know that.

Being nice means adding these types of activities to your children's daily routine:

- Paying someone a compliment.
- Smiling at people.
- Saying thank-you often.
- Doing someone a favor.
- Listening with more empathy.
- Being civil in all conversations.

- Seeking out and surrounding themselves with nice people.

Here's the way I like to think about what it means to be nice. Think about all the things you would like to have someone say about you at your funeral. You want them to say nice things about you, right? So teach your kids to be nice, and others will have no choice but to say those things about them.

Have them be known as people who are thoughtful, generous, kind, loving, polite, courteous, supportive, positive, faithful, and pleasant to be around. Teach them to always wear a smile. Those are the kinds of people they like to be around, so have them become one.

Habits are easy to form. They can get in the habit of being late or being on time. They can get into the habit of overeating or eating moderately. They can get into any habit—good or bad. Make up your mind to get your kids into good habits. Make up your mind to make them nice people! I think it was Abe Lincoln who said, "People are about as happy as they make up their minds to be." So teach them to make up their minds to be nice.

Make being nice the hallmark of all their interpersonal relationships. Some of those people they will like, others they will love, but all of them deserve niceness. Of course, they will treat family different from how they treat friends.

Of course, they will treat you different from the neighbors. Of course, they will treat their sisters different from how they treat their classmates. But they can at least be nice to all of them.

When they examine themselves to make sure that they still like that person in the mirror, make sure they assess whether or not they are being nice. Being nice will transform them, and, even more important, it will transform others. And if that's true, then it can transform America as well.

It goes without saying that teaching your kids to be nice is much easier when you're nice. Be their best example.

Law number three: Teach them to be nice.

Chapter 4

Getting to Know God

There are many different religions in the world. Most of them believe in some type of supreme being. But there are many people who do not believe in God.

Statistics show that approximately 16 percent of the world's population, just over one billion people, are either atheists or agnostics (www.adherents.com/Religions_By_Adherents .html). An atheist supposedly denies the existence of God, whereas an agnostic claims no knowledge of God but doesn't deny the possibility that God might exist.

The reason that I personally believe in God is related to design. If I told you that there was no designer of my house but that one day the wind just blew and the result was that my house appeared, you'd think I was crazy. We would both know that that wasn't true. The likelihood that the plumbing, electricity, carpentry, masonry, and painting all worked together so cohesively, without a designer or planner, is just incomprehensible to me.

Yet when I look at the complexity of the human body and the intricacies of the nervous system, cardiovascular/pulmonary system, reproductive system, digestive system, and so forth, I cannot help but conclude that there had to be a designer. I just don't believe that it all happened by chance.

As for me personally, I'm a born-again Christian. I totally trust in Jesus Christ as my Lord and Savior. But you need to decide for yourself what you believe. My advice is to genuinely and honestly seek the truth about God. I totally trust that God will reward that kind of genuine search and He will reveal Himself to you. I would read the Bible with the expectation that God will honor your search for Him. But you don't really find God; He finds you.

Some people view the Bible as a rulebook and they beat you up with it when you break their rules. Some denominations just seem to be against everything. But I view the Bible as a love letter from home. I see myself as an alien on earth. My true citizenship is in heaven.

The most incredible thing about God is that He wants to have a personal relationship with you and your children through His Son. He knows your name! He knows their names. Imagine that, to go through every day with a God that yearns for you and your children, and He knows your name.

I want to share a couple of stories with you and your children. The first one is about a room.

The Room

In that place between wakefulness and dreams, I found myself in the room. There were no distinguishing features except for the one wall covered with small index-card files. They were like the ones in libraries that list titles by author or subject in alphabetical order. But these files, which stretched from floor to ceiling and seemingly endless in each direction, had very different headings.

As I drew near the wall of files, the first to catch my attention was one that read, "Girls I Have Liked." I opened it and began flipping through the cards. I quickly shut it, shocked to realize that I recognized the names written on each one. And then without being told, I knew exactly where I was.

This lifeless room with its small files was a crude catalog system for my life. Here were written the actions of my every moment, big and small, in a detail my memory couldn't match. A sense of wonder and curiosity, coupled with horror, stirred within me as I began randomly opening files and exploring their content. Some brought joy and sweet memories; others brought a sense of shame and regret so intense that I would look over my shoulder to see if anyone was watching.

A file named "Friends" was next to one marked "Friends I Have Betrayed." The titles ranged from the mundane to the outright weird: "Books I Have Read," "Lies I Have Told," "Comfort I Have Given," "Jokes I Have Laughed At." Some were almost hilarious in their exactness, like "Things I've Yelled at My Brothers." Others I couldn't laugh at, such as "Things I Have Done in My Anger" and "Things I Have Muttered under My Breath at My Parents." I never ceased to be surprised by the contents. Often there were many more cards than I expected. Sometimes there were fewer than I hoped for. The sheer volume of the life I had lived overwhelmed me.

Could it be possible that I had the time in my years to fill each of these thousands or even millions of cards? But each card confirmed this truth. Each had been written in my own handwriting. Each was signed with my signature. When I pulled out the file marked "TV Shows I Have Watched," I realized the files grew to contain their contents. The cards were packed tightly and yet, after two or three yards, I hadn't found the end of the file. I shut it, shamed not so much by the quality of shows but more by the vast time I knew that that file represented.

When I came to a file marked "Lustful Thoughts," I felt a chill run through my body. I pulled the file out only an inch, not willing to test its size, and drew out a card. I shuddered at its detailed content. I felt sick to think that such a moment had been recorded. An almost animal rage broke on me. One thought dominated my mind: "No one must ever see these cards! No one must ever see this room! I have to destroy them!" In an insane frenzy, I yanked the file out. Its size didn't matter now. I had to empty it and burn the cards. But as I held it at one end and began pounding it on the floor, I could not dislodge a single card. I became desperate and pulled out a card, only to find it as strong as steel when I tried to tear it.

Defeated and utterly helpless, I returned the file to its slot. Leaning my forehead against the wall, I let out a long, self-pitying sigh. And then I saw it. The title said, "Times I've Spent Alone with God." The handle was brighter than those around it, newer, and almost unused. I pulled on its handle and a small box, not more than three inches long, fell into my hands. On one hand, I could count the cards it contained. And then the tears came. I began to weep. My sobs were so deep that they hurt. They started in my stomach and shook through me. I fell on my knees and cried. I cried out of shame, from the overwhelming shame of it all. The rows of file shelves swirled in my tear-filled eyes. No one must ever, ever know of this room. I must lock it up and hide the key. But then, as I pushed away the tears, *I saw Him.*

No, please not Him. Not here. Oh, anyone but Jesus. I watched helplessly as He began to open the files and read the cards. I couldn't bear to watch His response. And in the moments I could bring myself to look at His face, I saw a sorrow deeper than my own. He seemed to intuitively go to the worst boxes. Why did He have to read every one? Finally, He turned and looked at me from across the room. He looked at me with pity in His eyes. But this was a pity that didn't anger me. I dropped my head, covered my face with my hands, and began to cry again. He walked over and put His arm around me. He could have said so many things, but He didn't say a word. He just cried with me.

Then He got up and walked back to the wall of files. Starting at one end of the room, He took out a file and, one by one, began to sign His name over mine on each card. "No!" I shouted as I rushed to Him.

All I could find to say was, "No, no," as I pulled the card from Him. His name shouldn't be on these cards. But there it was, written in red so rich, so dark, and so alive. The name of Jesus covered mine. It was written with His blood. He gently took the card back. His mouth opened to a sad smile and He began to sign the cards. I don't think I'll ever understand how He did it so quickly, but the next instant it seemed I heard Him close the last file as He walked back to my side. He placed His hand on my shoulder and said, "It is finished."

I stood up, and He led me out of the room. There was no lock on the door. There are still more cards to be written.

That's the God we have. And He wants a personal relationship with you and your children.

I would now like to share a poem that I think reveals God's character and is worth sharing with your children. It was written by Sister Margaret Halaska.

The Covenant

God
knocks at the door of my heart,
seeking a home for His Son.

Rent is cheap, I say.

I don't want to rent. I want to buy, says God.

I'm not sure I want to sell,
But you can come in and look around.

I think I will, says God.

I might let you have a room or two.

I like it, says God. I'll take the two.
You might decide to give me more someday.
I can wait, says God.

I'd like to give you more,
But it's a bit difficult. I need some space for me.

I know, says God, I'll take it. I like what I see.

Hmm, maybe I can let you have another room.
I really don't need that much.

Thanks, says God, I'll take it. I like what I see.

I'd like to give you the whole house,
but I'm not sure …

Think on it, says God. I wouldn't put you out.
Your house would be mine and my Son would live in it.
You'd have more space than you ever had before.

I don't understand at all.

I know, says God, but I can't tell you about that.
You'll have to discover it for yourself.
That can only happen if you let me have the whole house.

A bit risky, I say.

Yes, says God, but try me!

I'm not sure …
I'll let you know.

I can wait, says God. I like what I see.

That is your God. He yearns for a personal relationship
with you. Our Founding Fathers had a deep faith rooted in
Christianity. God is on our money. The Ten Commandments
were once posted in every courtroom in America. Today
we see little of God in America. God is now banned from
our schools. We need to reclaim our heritage and stop
apologizing for being Christians. God was at the core of
America's foundation. But not anymore. Today it is not
politically correct to mention God. If there is one single
thing that has led to our nation's moral decline, I would say

that it is our abandonment of God. Our children need to become familiar with God.

Let me close with one of my favorite quotes. It is by Jim Elliot, a Christian missionary killed in 1956 in Ecuador evangelizing the Waodani people. He said, "He is no fool who gives what he cannot keep to gain that which he cannot lose." Spend time alone with God every day, and teach your children to do the same.

Law number four: Help your children get to know God.

Chapter 5

Doing unto Others:
The Gold in the Rule

Do unto others as you would have them do to you. That is the Golden Rule. It is the underlying law for all right and wrong. Jesus's version of that is simply to love your neighbor as yourself. They are similar and both are excellent rules. However one involves *doing* and the other involves *loving*. Both are laws that I would like for you to put on the lenses of your children.

It is easy to do good things for people who love you or who do good things for you. But what about that grouchy person next door? What about that bully at work? What about that person who blamed you when you were really innocent? It is much harder to do good for these people. But that is *not* the rule. The rule doesn't say to do back to them what they have done to you. That's called payback, revenge, or retribution. That's what our human nature says to do.

But the Golden Rule says to do to them what you would have them do to you. Ask your children to suppose for a minute that they were the bully. Have them suppose for a minute that they had told a lie about someone or been mean and ugly to someone. They might expect that person to be mean and ugly back to them because that's what they did to that person. After all, they would deserve it, right?

But what if the person they told a lie about didn't retaliate? What if instead he or she was nice to your child even after your child had been mean to him or her? How would your child feel then? Lousy, I bet. Your child would feel sorrow. Your child would feel regret. He or she might even feel like apologizing. It is important to play these situational games with your children. It forces them to see things from the other person's perspective.

So my suggestion is this: Tell your children to make others feel that way. Tell *your children* to be the nice guys. Tell them to remember that thing about being nice. Teach them to pay back with *good* what was done to them as *bad*, even when that's not what others may deserve. Show your children that, when they're nice and they treat others the way they want to be treated, even when the other person doesn't deserve it, it will make the other person feel lousy; it will make the other person feel the sorrow and regret.

Maybe the other person will even feel bad enough to apologize to your child. And if he or she does, and your child accepts the apology graciously, there may now even be the basis for a friendship. Imagine that—turning something *bad* into a *friendship*. All because your child didn't respond based on his or her human nature but rather on the Golden Rule.

Now here is the *gold in the rule:* that kid of yours is going to feel wonderful about him- or herself! When your child sees that person in the mirror tomorrow morning, he or she is going to love himself or herself. Your children are going to love themselves for who they are, what they did, and what they are becoming. And they will be proud. Everyone who knows them will be proud, most of all you.

When your children treat others well, it will undoubtedly be good for the people they help and are kind to, but they'll also notice a strange thing. People will start treating them better too. Beyond that, though, they will find a growing satisfaction with themselves, a belief in themselves, knowledge that they are good people and can trust in themselves.

We can even take this Golden Rule to a higher level. Until now we have only looked at the part of the Golden Rule that says don't pay back *in* kind, but pay back by *being* kind. Now we want to look beyond responding and look at initiating. But first, your child must understand the difference between mercy and grace.

Mercy is *not* getting what you deserve. Grace is *getting* what you *don't* deserve. Here is a simple example to share with your child. Suppose she gets stopped by a policeman for speeding. Suppose also that she is guilty. After talking with her, the officer decides not to give her a ticket but only a verbal warning. The officer has shown her mercy. He did not give her the ticket that she deserved.

Now suppose this same officer saw your child's bumper sticker and knows that she is a Georgia Bulldogs fan. Suppose he then gives her two free tickets to the next game because he can't go. The officer has now shown grace. He has given her something that she didn't deserve.

So by not giving your child a ticket, the policeman showed mercy, and by giving her the football tickets, he showed grace. When your child doesn't give somebody what he or she deserves *your child* is showing mercy. This is a big part of the Golden Rule. But there is more. What if your child went out of her way to perform some random act of kindness for someone? She would be showing grace. She would be giving or doing something for someone who didn't necessarily deserve it. This is also part of the Golden Rule. She is doing for someone else what she would like others to do for her.

I would like for you to ask your children to perform a random act of kindness for someone every day for two weeks. Open a door for an elderly person. Cut the neighbor's grass. Help someone with his homework. Clean someone's room without being asked. Fix dinner one night. There is so much gold in this rule. Test me on this. Have them perform one act of kindness every day for two weeks. And have them do it without expecting anything in return. Then after the two weeks, ask them how they feel about themselves. You'll be amazed!

Ask your children how they think all the recipients are going to feel after all these acts of kindness. They'll tell you that they are all going to feel very thankful. But do you know how good your children are going to feel about themselves? Do you know what they're going to feel when they see themselves in the mirror tomorrow morning? Just like that guy in the Men's Wearhouse commercial says, "You're going to like the way you look, I guarantee it!" That person in the mirror will start looking better and better to them every day.

There is a movie called *Pay It Forward* that stars Kevin Spacey, Helen Hunt, and Haley Joel Osment. In it, Trevor (Haley Joel Osment) and his class are given an assignment by their teacher (Kevin Spacey). The assignment is to think of something that would change the world. Trevor comes up with the idea that when someone does you a big favor, rather than paying them back you pay it forward to three other people. These would be random acts of kindness. And what do you think might happen in the world if, for every favor done for someone, three more were paid forward to other people? You're right—it would change the world. Teach your children to *pay it forward.*

I also remember a story about a little girl who lived next to a man whose wife had just died. The man was out on his front porch a week or so after the funeral and he was crying. The little girl went over and asked him why he was crying. He explained to her that his wife had died. After staying with him for a while, she went home and told her mother about visiting the man next door and about what had happened to his wife. The mother asked the little girl, "Well, honey, what did you do for him?" "Nothing," the little girl replied, "I just helped him cry." Sometimes all your children need to do to show kindness is to just show up.

Years ago, I was traveling on business in Brazil. One day, while I was having coffee at an outdoor café, a young boy about nine or ten years old came up to me. He didn't speak very good English, and I spoke no Portuguese, but it didn't take much sign language to figure out that he wanted to shine my shoes. I asked him how much he charged. In those days, the Brazilian currency was a *cruzeiro* and there was very high inflation. A dollar was worth about ten billion gazillion cruzeiros.

So he told me that a shoeshine cost ten billion gazillion cruzeiros. I frowned and told him that was *way* too much money. He was persistent and came back two or three more times. Finally, it dawned on me that we were only talking about a dollar. He was probably shining shoes, instead of being in school, so that he could help his parents feed his brothers and sisters. In exasperation, he came back one final time and said, "Senor, I shine shoes. You buy me food." And then he pointed inside to the restaurant. My heart melted and I felt about one inch tall. Needless to say, I bought him a lot of food. And I think I gave him the equivalent of 100 billion gazillion cruzeiros.

I'm not very proud of the way it all unfolded; it was not really a random act of kindness on my part. But I bet that night his mama thought it was.

My wife Sherrie is the epitome of someone doing random acts of kindness. Our housekeeper is Brazilian—see, I still must feel guilty—and she comes once each week to clean. Her name is Camilla and she has a daughter named Anna. Last year Anna was starting school. We learned that Anna had no school supplies, including no backpack or shoulder pack to carry them in.

The next day, Sherrie went to the store and bought Anna one of every school item it sold. The next week, Anna came with Camilla and Sherrie surprised them with the school supplies. They both cried. Then Sherrie and I cried. None of us will ever forget that day. And boy, did we look good in the mirror that next morning.

Life is filled with opportunities to commit random acts of kindness. One time I was at the grocery store behind a woman with several kids and she was paying for some of her items with food stamps. After the clerk had rung everything up, the lady was several dollars short. I could tell she was looking to see what she could put back. She looked at me a little embarrassed and then at the clerk. I handed the clerk a five-dollar bill without any hoopla and told her to give the change to the lady. The lady thanked me in a sheepish way and left with her kids. The clerk told me that it was very nice thing I had done. I just nodded. I wish I had told that lady to pay it forward.

The truth is that, on a day-to-day basis, living by the Golden Rule will make your children better people, will make those around them happier, and will make the community they live in a better place.

With that in mind, here are some practical ways your children can really put the Golden Rule into their daily lives:

- Practice empathy – have them really try to understand what other people are feeling.
- Practice compassion – when they see pain and suffering, tell them to do something about it.
- Be friendly – tell them to have a smile and a kind word for everyone.
- Be helpful – make sure they open a door for someone or unload the dishwasher.
- Be courteous in traffic – make sure they know to let people in. Don't let them become grumps when they get behind the wheel.
- Listen to others – don't just hear others but teach your children to really listen.

- Overcome prejudice – make sure they understand that "others" doesn't mean *some* others, it means *all* others.
- Minimize criticism – don't let them criticize unnecessarily. It is better for them to criticize from a love perspective than from an anger perspective.
- Send themselves reminders – have them set up recurring e-mail to themselves to remind them of the Golden Rule.
- Have them post it on their wall or make it their home page – tell them to put a reminder in places where they will see it every day.
- Always have them rise above retaliation – vengeance is done out of anger. Teach them that reconciliation is done out of love and compassion.
- Tell them to be the change – don't let them wait for others. Have them start today.
- Remind them to notice how it makes them feel – to pause and examine how they feel right after an act of kindness. It's incredible. They're going to love that person in the mirror.

There is a prayer on the Golden Rule, attributed to Eusebius of Caesarea, that is worth teaching to your children. It includes the following points, among others:

- May I gain no victory that harms me or my opponent.
- May I reconcile friends who are mad at each other.

- May I, insofar as I can, give all necessary help to my friends and to all who are in need.
- May I never fail a friend in trouble.

And make sure they know that forgiveness can be a part of the Golden Rule as well. Too many people harbor anger when forgiveness would be the better thing. And not just better for the person they are angry with, but sometimes forgiveness helps forgivers to get past a transgression and move on with their lives.

Several years ago, a man went inside a small Amish schoolhouse and killed almost a dozen children, and then he killed himself. In less than one week, the whole Amish community had forgiven the killer. And not only that, but over 50 percent of the people at the killer's funeral were Amish. In fact, they went even further and started a fund for the killer's wife and family. That is doing for others what you want others to do for you.

Sometime soon they might see a person in need. Or maybe it will be a homeless person. Who knows? Each of those will present an opportunity for your children to commit a random act of kindness—without expecting anything in return.

Law number five: Teach your children to obey the Golden Rule.

Chapter 6

Teach Them to Never Stop Learning

Never underestimate the value of an education. It will pay huge dividends over the course of your children's lives. Encourage them to stay in school as long as they can, to get as many degrees as they can, and to take all school seriously. Teachers and professors are there for *them*. Your children owe it to themselves and their teachers to give it their best effort. They will have the greatest success in education if they learn to love learning at an early age.

Education is so important and will make such a difference in their lives. When Aristotle was asked how much educated men were superior to those who were uneducated, Aristotle answered, "As much as the living are to the dead."

It is never hard to do what you want to do. When I quit smoking forty years ago, it was easy. Want to know why? *Because I wanted to be a nonsmoker more than I wanted a cigarette.* Same thing with dieting. When I wanted to be skinny more than I wanted food, it was no problem. Kate Moss said in 2009 that "Nothing tastes as good as thin feels." You never have trouble doing what you want to do. Your kids don't have any trouble having fun, do they? Know why? It's what they want to do.

The same thing is true with learning. When they *want* to learn, school and studying will be no problem because it will be what they want to do. Make it fun and make it enjoyable and make it last a lifetime. Frederick W. Robertson, a noted British educator of the 1800s, said, "Instruction ends in the classroom, but education ends only with life."

Reading is the fundamental key to all learning. Teach them how to read as early as possible. Have them read about everything. Read, read, and read some more. Every subject they will ever study in school will require reading. It is the single most important factor in learning.

What is the financial value of a great education? Statistics show that the higher your education, the more money you will make. According to the 2010 Bureau of Labor Statistics, Current Population Survey, the following is true:

- College graduates on average made $51,500 per year. Those with advanced degrees made $78,000 per year.
- Adults with a high school diploma earned $28,500 a year. See the difference a college degree makes?
- Adults who dropped out of high school earned $19,100 per year.
- 75 percent of future jobs will require a license or certificate.
- Occupations requiring a degree are projected to grow twice as fast as the national average for all occupations.
- The incremental lifetime earnings of a college graduate will be $1 million more than that of a high school graduate.

Those are some powerful statistics. It's hard to pass up on a college education when it means $1 million more than just a high school education. That's more than enough for them to send *their* kids to college. While money itself is not a particularly inspiring goal, having more money will add to the quality of life they will be able to provide for their families, including their children's education.

Teach them that education doesn't stop when they get out of school. They can learn something every day. They can learn something from everyone. When they're young, they will learn a tremendous amount from you, not just their teachers. But they can learn from friends, neighbors, relatives, books, the Internet, and on and on. There is no limit to the sources for learning. And through the Internet, the cost of obtaining an education is approaching zero. It could be that in their lifetime they will see the disappearance of public schools.

Also make sure they learn to develop a value system for life. Honesty, integrity, and respect for individuals are cornerstones to real wisdom. As they display their value system to the world through their ordinary day-to-day living, they will be teaching those around them about happiness, cooperation, simplicity, love, unity, peace, and humility.

It is the students' desire to know that impels education. It is their curiosity, their creativeness, their inquisitiveness, their own motivation, and their desire that will determine how educated and wise they will become. The poet William Butler Yeats said, "Education is not the filling of a pail, but rather the lighting of a fire." Your children are in control of their own education. Let their fire burn brightly. Tell them to seek to fulfill their potential. Teach them to take the initiative. It's for them; they might as well do their best.

I hope you now realize the importance of a good education for your children and that learning never ends. Sometimes, however, their education may not receive the proper priority. Consider the following simple little diagram.

	Important	Not Important
Urgent	A	B
Not Urgent	C	D

Quadrant A contains all the things in life that are both urgent and important. These things are usually top priority because they are both urgent and important. Things like accidental injuries, when you cut your hand, would be considered urgent. Your health and safety are important, and the bleeding is urgent. It must be addressed right away.

All the things in quadrant D represent the lowest priorities in life because they are neither urgent nor important. An example is changing the oil in the car. It's not urgent, and, based on other priorities, it may not be really important either.

Quadrant B is trickier. While these things are not important, they are urgent and somehow demand our immediate attention. Perhaps a water pipe breaks in the house. It's not really important, but it certainly is urgent. These things get quickly resolved because they're urgent.

And now we come to the all-important quadrant C of the square. These are the things that are important, but they aren't urgent. The tendency is to put these off because they're *not* urgent. But the problem with putting them off is that they're *important*. Education fits in this quadrant. It's *very* important, but it never appears to be urgent. Make sure to help your kids identify quadrant C activities, and never let them forget how important the activities are to their future.

We live in a world today that is overly focused on the urgent. Never let the important things for your children become subordinate to the urgent. Not only does education live here, but all the other important things in their lives that aren't urgent live here as well. Regular visits to the doctor for annual physicals, exercising, spending time with the family, helping a friend, taking time to relax and doing something fun, and getting to know God are just a few.

Have your kids make their own list of what is important to them. You can add a few things for them as well. You and your children should check the list regularly to make sure that these important things are receiving the attention they deserve.

Law number six: Teach them to never stop learning

Chapter 7

Make Sure They Learn to Make a Difference

No matter how bad things may seem in your children's life, they will always be able to find someone in worse shape. There is an old saying, "I used to complain that I had no shoes, until I met a man who had no feet." No matter how hungry kids are, or how poor they are, there are people out there hungrier and poorer. And they need our help.

Jesus said, "Love your neighbor as yourself" (Luke 10:27). And man, is that hard to do. This statement goes beyond the Golden Rule, because doing to others what you want them to do to you does not involve love. But, at a bare minimum, we can at least help those people who need help.

If your child's car breaks down and he's stranded on the side of the road, wouldn't you want someone to help him? Of course, you would. Then the next time he sees a motorist stranded on the side of the road, what should he do? Sure, he should help the motorist out. He can call 911 and have help sent. If your child takes algebra in school, or perhaps chemistry, and there are some things that he just doesn't understand, wouldn't you like for someone to help him? If so, then teach your child to find someone at school who needs some tutoring.

It is almost a certainty that if children develop the discipline of helping people regularly, they will eventually come across people who don't appreciate it. Some might think they're interfering; some might be too embarrassed to admit they need help; others might even get angry. Tell your kids not to let this deter them. Have them continue to help people—it's just the right thing to do.

And let me tell you one other important thing that will happen to them. They are going to feel really good about themselves. When they feel really good about themselves, do you know what else happens? Remember chapter one? They are going to absolutely love that person in the mirror. I may have already mentioned that I have a friend who has a great tagline on all his e-mails. It says, "Do the right thing. And do it right now!" Helping other people is just the right thing to do. So tell your kids to do it the minute they see the need or opportunity.

Helping people will become a habit. I suggest that they start by trying to help someone every day. Maybe it's just emptying the dishwasher, or cleaning their rooms, cutting the grass, studying with a friend, or loaning somebody lunch money at school. It could be anything they choose. As they get older, they will have many more options from which to choose. They can volunteer to work at hospitals, libraries, or nursing homes. They can get involved with charitable organizations like the Red Cross, Habitat for Humanity, the Salvation Army, or any number of organizations that are important to them.

Many of your children are old enough to remember September 11, 2001, when the United States was attacked by terrorists who flew commercial airplanes into the World Trade Center in New York City and the Pentagon in Washington, DC. On that day, the first responders, largely the firefighters and police officers, went to work immediately to help others in need. Now you could argue that they were helping because that was their job, and to some degree that might be true. But they were selfless and genuine in their efforts to help people on that day.

And yet on that day, a greater phenomenon occurred. Thousands of normal citizens banded together to help one another. It didn't matter what religion they had, what their societal status was, their skin color, their gender or sexual orientation, or their nationality. People just started helping other people any way they could. It was a heart-warming thing to behold. What if we could harness the spirit that existed that day and teach our children to demonstrate that behavior and live that way every day? I believe it would change the world. It can, and must, start with you and your children.

There is a variety of benefits to your children by helping others. Some of them are as follows:

- It will make them happy and make them feel good about themselves.
- It will build trust as others see they have no ulterior motive for helping them.
- It will come back to them; I can't explain how this works, but it does, so have them try it.
- It improves the community and society in general.
- It will make them feel connected to people.
- It will make them feel generous, needed, and effective.
- It will take their minds off their worries for a while.
- It will give them a sense of meaning and purpose in life.

In the end, one of the biggest reasons for your children to help others is because it will leave their mark on the world. When they help others, they live on in the memories of those they helped. They've made a difference in someone's life.

Think about your child teaching someone, who otherwise would still be illiterate, to read. Do you know what a gift that would be? Do you know how much difference that would make in a person's life? I've taught illiterate adults to read. It's like introducing them to a whole new world. It's like giving sight to the blind.

Having your children leave their mark on the world is huge. Making a difference is more important than making money. Wouldn't it make you feel awesomely proud to know that your child made a positive difference in someone's life? Teaching this concept to your children might be the biggest difference *you* make in this world. Somebody taught it to Mother Teresa, and look what a difference she made!

Law number seven: Make sure they learn to make a difference.

Chapter 8

Eating Healthy and Staying Fit

I know that most of your children are probably not overweight or out of shape. But trust me, that won't always be the case. When I was in high school, I played football, basketball, and baseball. I was in pretty good shape. As I got older and less active, and as my metabolism decreased, I began to put on weight. I got up to 250 pounds.

One day I read an article about a guy who had just run a marathon. He said in his article, "I know now that it is possible to accomplish anything through sheer force of will, because I have run a marathon." I thought it was powerful, kind of a mind-over-matter thing. So the next day, I bought a pair of running shoes and started training. The first time on the track, I could only run one lap. A marathon is 105 laps. I distinctly remember saying to myself, "It is only my first day, and already I can run 1/105th of the distance. This attitude is a far cry from, "I can hardly run one lap, let alone 105."

But that was my attitude. I kept at it week after week. I had quit smoking, started a diet, and started training. Ninety days later, I entered the Atlanta Marathon on Thanksgiving Day. I was not very prepared but I wanted to try. I got twenty-one miles before my legs just ran out of gas. I had to quit. But I wasn't discouraged. In ninety days, I had gone from one lap to eighty-four. The next Thanksgiving, I completed the marathon in three hours and twenty-eight minutes. That is under eight minutes a mile, which is pretty fast for someone weighing two hundred pounds.

At the peak of my training I weighed one hundred ninety pounds and I was running around fifty miles each week. I ran several more marathons and my best time was two hours, fifty-four minutes. That is about six minutes and forty seconds per mile, which was very fast for my size, but at that time it was not fast enough to qualify for the Boston Marathon.

So I stopped running marathons and over the next year I wasn't running anymore at all. Guess what happened. I gained all the weight back. When I was running fifty miles every week, I could eat whatever I wanted and as much as I wanted. But when I stopped running and didn't change my diet, I gained the weight right back. The same thing will happen to you and your kids.

As you know, when children get older their metabolism slows down and they don't burn calories at the same rate as when they were young. Like most people my age, I see this as totally unfair. But that's the way it is.

If you have your health, you have a lot. Never let your kids take that for granted. I was running so much that it became unhealthy for me. I had a stress fracture in my lower left leg and I was experiencing blood in my urine. The marathon itself was not the culprit, but training fifty miles per week was just too much for my body, especially considering my size. When I was injured and couldn't train, I was miserable. I had taken my ability to run for granted. When I couldn't run, I realized how important my health really was to me.

There are three components to staying healthy that kids must know:

1. Exercise regularly.
2. Eat a healthy diet.
3. Get regular checkups with the doctor.

Working Out

There are literally thousands of books and videos about exercising. And I don't mean to belittle their value, but it is really not all that complicated. There are only three components that your children need to know.

Cardio

First is cardiovascular training. This is basically getting the heart rate up to about 75 percent of its maximum and keeping it there for thirty to forty minutes.

They can do this by running (on the street or on a treadmill), biking, rowing, swimming, participating in a cardio class at the gym, walking up stairs, or anything else that gets them breathing hard and makes them sweat. The key is to do it for thirty to forty minutes. Don't worry about the pace. They should start slow and build up gradually. Their heart rate should be their guide for setting the pace. Go at whatever pace is required to keep the heart rate around 75 percent of their maximum. The heart rate guidelines vary by age, and the maximum heart rate declines as they get older. The general rule of thumb is that your maximum heart rate (MHR) should equal 220 minus your age. So if your child is sixteen, his or her MHR would be approximately 204. Specific tables of MHR can be easily found on the Internet.

I suggest that they do a cardio workout three to four times each week. Varying the exercise will not only keep them from getting bored, but it will use different muscles in the process.

Resistance

The second aspect of exercise is resistance training, or weight training. I recommend weight training three times per week, but always with a day off in between. Muscles grow faster and stronger with ample time to rest and recover between workouts. They should do an upper-body workout (arms, chest, back) one day and a lower-body workout (quadriceps, hamstrings, calves, and glutes) the next time.

The last part of the weight training is for the core. This involves the abdominal area and lower back. These are typically exercises that can be done without expensive equipment. They can do sit-ups and/or leg raises and use inexpensive items like medicine balls, Swiss balls, elastic bands, steps, and jump ropes.

Stretching

The third and final type of exercise I recommend for your children is stretching. A flexible body greatly reduces the likelihood of injury. But tell them to be careful about stretching cold muscles. Warm muscles stretch better. So it is best to do light exercise for a little while and then stretch. The best time to stretch is at the end of the workout. Their muscles are good and warm and they will get the maximum flexibility benefit from the stretch. When stretching, teach them to try to hold the maximum stretch for twenty seconds. Don't let them bounce—stretch and hold. The most important things to keep flexible, in my experience, are the lower back and hamstrings.

Make sure that they also do something fun. While not a workout per se, have them play tennis, join a softball team or a bowling league, or play volleyball—something that keeps them active and that they enjoy. Don't make their exercise something they hate; plan lots of variety. Give them permission to take a day off once in a while, and always try to have them take one day of complete rest every week.

Diet

Just like with exercise, there are thousands of books about dieting. The reason for that is that Americans are fat but don't want to be, so they buy books looking for quick and easy answers. There are no quick and easy answers to obesity. The best way to avoid being overweight is to start eating correctly at an early age, like your kids are right now.

It isn't rocket science. Make them eat a balanced diet. That is, a diet with protein (meat for most people, but other sources for vegetarians), fruits, vegetables, fat, and carbohydrates (pasta, rice, potatoes). Their bodies needs some fat, but try to limit their fat intake. Also, make sure they watch their calorie intake. Desserts and sweets are very fattening. I also recommend drinking plenty of water, especially when they're exercising but other times as well. Sweet drinks like sodas and sweet tea are high in calories.

All in all, they should eat a little bit of everything. Don't deny them a treat once in a while. Here is what I do every day. I weigh myself first thing in the morning. If I'm one pound higher than I want to be, I watch what I eat that day.

If my weight is good, I eat a sensible, balanced diet with dessert if I want it. That way I'll never be more than one pound overweight!

Usually, if I have bread at lunch, I won't have potatoes with dinner, and vice versa. I try to eat more fish and chicken than beef and pork, but I don't abstain from any of them. Make sure they learn to like salads, which are great for them.

If they do get overweight, encourage them to lose it right away. The older they get, the harder it will be to lose weight. Don't let them go on fad diets or diets that promise large and rapid weight loss. They didn't gain the weight overnight so don't let them lose it overnight. The best way is to not let them think they're on a diet at all. Tell them to think about it as changing their eating habits for life. Make their new way of eating their lifestyle, not their diet.

Regular Checkups

When kids are young and under twenty years old, they really only need to go to the doctor when they're sick or don't feel well or when they know something isn't right with their bodies. If they listen to their bodies, they will know when something is just not quite right.

After age twenty, my rule is this: they should go to the doctor for regular checkups twice in their twenties, three times in their thirties, four times in their forties, and so on. The older they get, the more often they should get regular checkups. The biggest indicator of overall health is blood chemistry. In addition, the doctor will advise things like chest X-rays, electrocardiograms, and colonoscopies at periodic times. Always have them follow the doctor's advice.

After age twenty, it is also good for them to check their blood pressure regularly to make sure it is in the normal range. High blood pressure over a prolonged period can cause big problems, not the least of which is kidney disease.

The most important reason for regular checkups is that most illnesses and diseases are treatable if caught early. An ounce of prevention is worth more than a pound of cure.

My mother is a perfect example of what *not* to do. She died at age sixty-six. She smoked a pack of unfiltered cigarettes every day of her life, she never exercised (although she was never overweight), and her diet was horrible. My mother would put butter in the pan before cooking bacon. Her cholesterol was nearly four hundred. She died suddenly from a cerebral hemorrhage. We had all pleaded with her to change her lifestyle, but she didn't. In essence, she made us watch her commit suicide. Her death was very predictable. My poor father had to live another twenty years without her. Don't do that to your family, and teach your kids likewise. Someday they will hopefully have spouses and children of their own. Teach them to stay healthy, not just for themselves but for the sake of their future families.

In closing, I would just like to say that there are other physicians besides the family doctor whom your kids should see on a regular basis. Visiting the eye doctor, dentist, and other specialists as required are all advised. And for your young ladies, a mammogram and a Pap smear at regular intervals are recommended.

If they remain healthy and fit, the *quality* of their life will be better as well as the *longevity*.

Law number eight: Teach them to eat healthy and stay fit.

Chapter 9

All Work and No Play Sucks: Have Them Go for Balance

Just like their diets should be balanced, their lifestyles should be balanced as well. There is an old saying, "All work and no play makes Jack a dull boy." But let me tell you that *too much of anything* is not good for you.

One of my biggest faults is a lack of balance in my life. My tendency is to be focused on one thing at a time, to the detriment of everything else. I struggle with it every day. Today is a perfect example. I'm sitting here at my computer writing this book. I'm focused. I'm locked in. Everything else is tuned out. I will probably not exercise today, but I should. I will probably not read a book today, but I should. I will probably not sit down to just relax today, but I should. See what I mean? If I were balanced, I would make time for each of them every day.

In an earlier chapter, I discussed the C quadrant of a four-square diagram—the section where all the nonurgent and important things live. Have your kids make a list of those things that are important to them and make sure that they make time for them every day.

My advice is to have them make time for seven things every day. And remember that this advice is falling on my own ears as well. I will list these in order of priority for me. Your priority and their priorities may be different, and the time spent on each one may be different from mine, but spend time on each of them every day.

1. Alone time with God – it can be early or late, but it is best at one of these two extremes. Either start your day with Him or end it with Him. I recommend a time of Bible reading, prayer, and listening to Him. Be still. Meditate on Him. My relationship with God is the most important thing in my life. In a previous chapter, I suggested your children get to know Him. Once they do, spending time alone with Him will become a priority.

2. Family – except for weekends, this is usually done in the evenings. These are the people your kids love most in the world. Spend quality time together. Get to know each other, trust each other, and understand each other. If done in the right quantity, this will leave little time for television. That's a good thing.

3. Work or school – in order to enjoy life, it takes a certain amount of money for even the daily necessities. Their

jobs, or their work, will be what provides the income for enjoying everything else. Have them put in the time. Tell them to be good students and the best employees. Make sure they give 110 percent effort at school and at work. Teach them to earn their pay. And when they leave work, leave work. Don't let them take it home. Same with school. If they're students, then giving 110 percent at school is fine, but after school tell them to go have some fun.

4. Sleep – it is critical for your children to get a good sleep every night. Sleep is essential to their overall health. It rejuvenates them. Their brains and bodies work hard all day. Give them the rest that they need. If they don't sleep well for a prolonged period, take them to see a doctor because something is wrong.

5. Exercise – in the previous chapter, I talked about the importance of staying fit. Make time for exercise in their daily schedules. Alberto Salazar, a great marathon runner, said, "If I take a day off from training I can notice it. If I take two days off my competitors notice it. If I take three days off everybody notices it." Don't let them take too many days off.

6. Relax – make sure they take a little time each day just to decompress. Have them drink a glass of tea or a cup of coffee and chat with a friend or family member about their day. Facebook and Twitter are fun things for kids and help them relax. Make sure they include laughter in this relaxation time—it is the great elixir of the soul.

7. Read – reading is important for your children because it is the key ingredient to education and learning. It

can also be a way for them to relax, fulfill a hobby, or escape reality for a little while. Reading will keep them current with the world and informed on the issues of the day.

If I were to allocate time for these seven activities across a twenty-four-hour day, here is how I would do it. (For you and your children, it may be different.)

- Time alone with God   1 hour
- Family   3 hours
- Work/school   10 hours
  (includes commute)
- Sleep   7 hours
  (some people need more)
- Exercise   1 hour
- Relax   1 hour
- Read   1 hour

It just sucks to do too much of any one thing over a prolonged period. Make sure they find a balance in life, and make the appropriate time for the things that are important to them.

Law number nine: Teach them to keep balance in their lives.

Chapter 10

Money Matters

Money isn't the only thing in the world. But some people say that it's way ahead of whatever's second. I think it was Pearl Bailey, a black singer, actress, and comedian who said, "I've been rich and I've been poor. Rich is better." It is going to take money for your kids to get along in this world. Even though they're young, they've probably already figured that out.

But there is a lot more to learn about money than just spending it. My guess is that they already know how to do that pretty well. So I want to give you a little money advice to pass on to them because it will matter a lot when they get older.

The first basic concept is a budget. They must know how much money they get every month and they must know how much money they must spend every month. They should write all this down. Have them make two lists: a list of their income sources and a list of their expenses. Let's say they have one hundred dollars of income every month and sixty-five dollars in expenses every month. This means that, after they pay all their bills, they will have thirty-five dollars left.

They should never let their expenses exceed their income because then they won't be able to pay all their bills. So when their expenses start to approach their income, they need to stop spending. This is teaching them to live within their means, also known as the budgeting process. They must know their income and expenses and how much they spend for certain things each month.

Some people don't budget very well and their expenses exceed their income. Sometimes they then borrow money to pay their bills. Many times people use credit cards to do this. My advice to your children is to never buy anything that they can't pay for. If they can't afford it, then they should save until they can. The only thing I recommend your kids borrow money for is to buy a house. For everything else, they should pay cash. Even for a car.

It will be tempting for them to borrow money for things. Don't let them do it. It's called debt. It means they will owe people. The people who want to loan them money will make it easy for them to pay it back, just a little at a time. But they charge interest. If they lend them ten dollars, they want your child to pay back eleven dollars. They may let your child pay one dollar per month for eleven months, and it sounds like a great deal. It's enticing. Don't let them do it. It's a trap.

There are adults who borrowed to have the things that they wanted. They weren't willing to save until they had enough money to pay cash. They wanted it *now*. Lenders made it easy for them to have it now. Many of these people have borrowed so much that now they can't pay it back. They don't make enough money. They have payments for houses, cars, flat-screen TVs, furniture, and credit cards. Some people have eight or ten credit cards with a $5,000 balance on each one. They can't even afford to pay the interest. Don't let your children be borrowers. Teach them to be savers. They can buy the items when they have the money.

I think it's okay for them to use a credit card for convenience purposes, as long as they pay the balance off every month and avoid paying interest.

The next thing I recommend to your kids is saving 10 percent of everything they make. I would begin at five years old and have them save 10 percent of everything they got, even the five dollars their grandmother gave them for their fifth birthday. If they're already over five years old and they don't have this habit, then start teaching them today.

Teach them the magic of compound interest. If they save one hundred dollars and leave it in a savings account that pays 2 percent interest, then next year they will have $102. Let's say that in the next year they save another hundred dollars. In that year, they will earn 2 percent on the $102 as well as 2 percent on the additional hundred dollars. They earn interest on their interest. With compound interest, if they save ten dollars each week beginning at age ten, at 3 percent compound interest, then at age sixty-five they will have over $70,000. Now that's a lot of mullah, baby! So get them early in the habit of saving 10 percent of everything they receive.

Everyone needs to plan for his or her financial future. People will have cars and houses to buy, children to rear, college to pay for, and a retirement to fund. The time to start saving for those things is today. Then when the need arises, they will have the money. Plus they will always be hit by unplanned emergencies that require money. It will be a great comfort to know that they have a financial cushion at those times.

The next thing I recommend is for your children to give 10 percent of everything they get to charity. This is what God instructs us to do in the Bible. We all come into this world with nothing. And we all leave this world with nothing. Everything we have in the interim God entrusts to us to manage. Since He provides it all, and because it's not really ours, He only asks for 10 percent back. That's a reasonable request in my opinion. And it makes me feel good to give something back. It makes me like that person in the mirror.

Suppose I give your child a ten-dollar bill and ask her to hold on to it for me. Suppose an hour later I asked her to give that same ten-dollar bill to you. Do you think she would have any problem doing that? Probably not. Do you know why? Because she never really thought of it as her money anyway. It is never hard to give something to another when it was never yours to begin with. That's the way I think about money. It's all God's money. None of it is really mine. So I don't mind giving God's money away.

I have some friends who try to live on as little as possible so they can give more away. It is a tremendous feeling to know that you have helped someone else. Teach your children to give to charities. They can give to their church and they can give directly to people they know who are in need. They can give in any number of ways.

In the book of Malachi, the last book of the Old Testament, God challenges His people to bring their tithe (that is, 10 percent) into the storehouse so that there will be food in the temple. God then says something unique: "Test me in this matter, to see if I will not open for you the windows of heaven and pour out for you blessings until there is no room for it all." Now that is quite a promise.

I decided to test the Lord as He suggested. I started giving 10 percent of everything I made to Him even when bills went unpaid. Today my house is paid for, my cars are paid for, and I have no credit card or other debt of any kind. And I have enough money saved to last me the rest of my life. If you haven't done this already, test God for yourself and see what happens.

So if your children save 10 percent and give 10 percent away, then that means that their budgets must allow them to pay all their bills on 80 percent of their income. Sounds hard, but it's just a habit. Get them into that habit early.

Once they have saved a reasonable amount of money, they may choose to invest in the stock market through individual stocks or mutual funds. Investing can earn much more than compound interest, but it is also risky so they can lose money as well. Before investing, make sure they seek the advice of a financial planner. It may be someone they know and you, as parents, can probably help them as well.

I would also recommend that at an early age they open checking accounts. They should have had a savings account since they were five, but if they don't have one, open these accounts for them at the same time they open their checking accounts. Teach them how to balance a checkbook. Teach them the responsibility of managing their money. Review their bank statements with them. Make sure they understand the details of it. Teach them about debit cards, online banking, and writing checks. After all, it's their money.

One final financial recommendation that I would make to your children is about lending money to others. My experience is that if it can be avoided, then avoid it. I would advise them to help those people find another source of money. Lending money can ruin a great friendship. I've seen it happen.

If they have developed the habit of saving early, then it won't take others long to figure out that, if they need money, they should come to your kid. So your kids should expect it. Remind them that they are not obligated to lend to anyone. It is important for them to know that they should never feel bad if they choose not to lend money to someone.

There will be occasions however when they want to lend money. It may be to a close friend or someone who has an emergency. They will have to make a decision about whether or not they trust the person to pay it back. My advice to them is this: if your child needs the money back, then don't lend it.

Oftentimes, people don't repay their loans even though they have the best of intentions. This will put your child in a bind if the money is not paid back by the time they need it. But if they don't need the money back (obviously they *want* it back) and they feel good about the person, then go ahead and lend the money. Whether they charge them interest or not is up to them and will probably depend on the circumstances.

So there you have it—teach your kids to save 10 percent, give 10 percent away, and not go into debt for anything except a house. Teach them about budgeting, how to balance a checkbook, and how to be smart about investing and lending, and they'll be just fine.

Law number ten: Teach them about money matters.

Chapter 11

They Are Special

There is a story about a little girl who said, "I know I'm somebody special, 'cause God don't make no junk!" She couldn't have been more right. Your children are special, and don't ever let anyone tell them different. I want you to put a law on their lenses right now that says, "I will determine my own self-worth and I am of great value."

Their self-worth is not dependent on anything else. It is not external; it is decided by them. No one can make them feel inferior without their permission. Their self-worth is certainly not dependent on anything external. It is not dependent on their looks, their brains, their jobs, their cars, their money, their athletic ability, their winning, or their report cards. They determine their self-worth. Teach them that today, and never let them give an inch on that position.

They are special people. They are valuable. They are unique. God made them for Himself.

They are of such great worth that God would rather die than live without them. That was the purpose of Christ's death on the cross. He provided a pathway to heaven that grants us eternal life. If the Creator of the universe would die for them, then they must be pretty special.

There are many reasons why self-worth is critical for your children:

- Self -worth can be the difference between success and failure.
- Self-worth affects their thinking, causing their outlook to be positive or negative.
- Self-worth affects their confidence.
- Self-worth affects their self-image.
- When they do not value themselves, they cannot value others.
- Self-worth enables them to have the right attitude to succeed at work and school.
- Self-worth is directly correlated to their happiness.

No matter when or where they embark on their personal journey of discovery, remember to always tell your children that they are *worth* it. *They* are the ones who are in charge of establishing it, and *they* are the ones who must endorse and project it.

When they recognize their innate worth, they are more inclined to strive to fulfill their potential and thereby create their own happiness. Successful people exude a sense of confidence in themselves. They realize that they are the directors of their own destinies, and therefore they take positive stances as they look forward.

The first step in acknowledging and accessing their worth, value, and sense of fulfillment is to make an honest personal assessment of themselves. An assessment of who they are and where they stand is vital to their ability to function freely in the world. By assessing and recognizing their abilities, they validate themselves. They need to do that in order for others to validate them.

Without personal awareness of their abilities, goals, and challenges, your children can lose sight of their choices. Teach them to resist the urge to blindly accept what others say about them and they will experience an enormous sense of freedom.

Never underestimate the importance of self-worth. What your children feel about themselves shows up in everything that they do and everything that they are willing to undertake. An acceptance of themselves, that they are worthy, has to be achieved so that they can believe that others see their value.

When your children form any kind of relationship, if they do not feel worthy of being in the same company then they will not gain other people's respect, and the relationship will probably fail. Feeling worthy of themselves can be the difference between success and failure in personal relationships.

You rarely see a performer on stage who does not feel worthy of playing to the audience. You rarely see an athlete who does not feel he or she is worthy of being among the other competitors. No matter how proficient or competent they are, self-worth is an underlying factor in anything a person attempts. Without self-worth, your children will have feelings of inferiority that will be a definite barrier to their success.

Maybe you read the book or saw the movie entitled *The Help*. It was written by Kathryn Stockett and it takes place in Mississippi in the 1960s. There is a black woman named Aibileen who is a maid for a wealthy white family. Part of Aibileen's duties included taking care of the family's children. The maids acted as surrogate mothers, including breastfeeding the white babies. The biological white mother had little time for her daughter. Aibileen frequently told the little girl, "You is kind. You is smart. You is important." Aibileen definitely knew something about self-worth and how important it is to small children.

Remember this: the important thing to understand is your children can think anything they want about themselves. It is their thoughts that determine their destinies. They are the ones who get to decide whether to listen to those who might eat away at their confidence and try to make them feel worthless. They get to decide whether to feel worthy of themselves or to continually let others eat away at their own self-worth.

Sometimes other kids can be cruel. They can make your child feel like an outsider, like he's not part of the group. They can make him feel like there is something wrong with him. It is a natural tendency to believe others, particularly if he's hearing it from more than one person. When that happens, tell him to look in the mirror. If he likes the person whom he sees, then ignore those other kids. Tell him to rest in the assurance that he is a good and valuable person. If he's done something or said something that he doesn't like about himself, then tell him to go fix it. Don't let him ever blindly believe what somebody else thinks about him. Other people are not the authority. Your child can see himself in the mirror. He is the authority; he is the only honest judge of himself.

Peer pressure is also a powerful thing. Your children will experience it. They will be in situations where the easy thing is to go along with the crowd. Perhaps they will be tempted to do things that they know are wrong, perhaps even things that are illegal. During those times, they need to remember that they don't need to go along with the crowd to feel good about themselves. They don't have to go along to be popular. They are already of great value. They don't need confirmation from others. They will know that they are worthy because you will have taught that to them.

Remember that each of your children is going to face that person in the mirror tomorrow. And what that person thinks about himself is far more important than what others think about him!

Law number eleven: Teach them that they are special.

Epilogue

So why are these eleven things so important? They are essential to your children's fulfillment, to them becoming the best that they can be. But these are also the essential and most fundamental things upon which our country was founded. And over the last two hundred years or so, our country has abandoned them. Losing these eleven things is the root cause of what's wrong with America today.

We have tons of problems in America. We have enormous debt, a spending addiction, entitlement programs that are unsustainable, borders we can't protect, an epidemic of fatherlessness, drug cartels, rampant pornography, energy issues, and on and on. We've created a big mess, and we've left it for our children. We should have done better. They are our last hope.

But I believe that if we can get these eleven laws on the lenses of our children, then over time they will solve all these other problems. Problems don't fix themselves. It takes people with great character and great integrity to fix a broken country. It takes people like our kids!

I don't believe in treating the symptom. I believe in treating the cause. I believe that if I had a magic wand and could wave it across all of our American children, instantly placing these eleven laws on their lenses, America would be just fine. But I don't have a magic wand. What I have is you. And because being comes before doing, I need you to *be* a great parent before I can ask your children to *do* something great. I believe that these eleven laws, once embodied by our children, will make them the great people who are needed to fix our nation.

It all starts with you. It's not about other people. It's about us—*we* the people. Are you bold enough to put these eleven laws on the lenses of your children? What? Don't think they can make any difference? Let me close with a story.

There was an older man sitting on the beach one morning. And far in the distance, he could see a young man who looked like he was dancing. As the old man moved closer, he realized that the young man wasn't dancing at all but was picking something off the beach and throwing it back into the ocean. Finally, he reached the young man and asked him what he was doing.

"I'm throwing these starfish in the ocean. The sun is coming up soon, and these starfish will all die." As the old man surveyed the beach, he could see that there were thousands of starfish. He turned to the young man and said, "There are thousands of starfish. You can't possibly make a difference." The young man bent down, picked up another starfish, and threw it in the ocean. He turned to the old man and said, "I made a difference for that one."

You too can make a difference!

Don't be an observer in the universe; be a participant. Make a difference. America needs your children. Think what might happen if each of us saved just one starfish!

About the Author

Steve White is a management consultant specializing in thought management and helping companies develop visions and strategic business plans for their organizations. He is the author of *Please Change Your Mind*, a self-help book about examining your thoughts. He enjoys tennis and lives in Atlanta, Georgia, with his wife, Sherrie, and their cat, Cashmere. You can visit him at his website at www.SteveWhiteToday.com.